T0116836

A Senior's Guide to Fall Prevention and Healthy Living

Roxanne Reynolds

BALBOA.
PRESS

A DIVISION OF HAY HOUSE

Balboa Press books may be ordered through booksellers or by contacting:

Balboa Press
A Division of Hay House
1663 Liberty Drive
Bloomington, IN 47403
www.balboapress.com
1-(877) 407-4847

Because of the dynamic nature of the Internet, any web addresses or links contained in this book may have changed since publication and may no longer be valid. The views expressed in this work are solely those of the author and do not necessarily reflect the views of the publisher, and the publisher hereby disclaims any responsibility for them.

The author of this book does not dispense medical advice or prescribe the use of any technique as a form of treatment for physical, emotional, or medical problems without the advice of a physician, either directly or indirectly. The intent of the author is only to offer information of a general nature to help you in your quest for emotional and spiritual well-being. In the event you use any of the information in this book for yourself, which is your constitutional right, the author and the publisher assume no responsibility for your actions.

Any people depicted in stock imagery provided by Thinkstock are models, and such images are being used for illustrative purposes only. Certain stock imagery © Thinkstock.

ISBN: 978-1-4525-4040-5 (sc)
ISBN: 978-1-4525-4041-2 (e)

Library of Congress Control Number: 2011918357

Printed in the United States of America

Balboa Press rev. date: 10/28/2011

Contents

Great tips on providing a safer home. We spend most of our time at home and this is where most falls take place.

Chapter 2. Body & Health 15

Tips and ideas on ways to improve your physical and mental health. Our energy comes from getting enough rest, having a healthy mindset, drinking clean water, eating fresh foods and exercise.

Chapter 3. Care Of Your Feet .42

Covers one of the most neglected parts of the body - our feet, which are most often abused from improper footwear and poor circulation.

Chapter 4. Check It Out 50

Outline of a number of diseases and afflictions associated with falls. If you have one of these your chances of falling rises.

Chapter 5. Living Well 74

The human body is designed for movement. Without it the muscles atrophy, circulation slows down and bones begin to thin. There are many applications, techniques, therapies, and classes offered to help maintain good posture and balanced movement. You may choose to try more than one depending on your physical ability. Do what "feels" right to you.

Chapter 6. Your Senses. 106

This section covers obvious changes that occur as we age and the role they play in relationship to our balance.

Chapter 7. Body, Mind & Spirit 113

Want more clarity, lessening of stress and a general sense of well being? What about better posture and breathing habits? You can have all this and much more through a Body, Mind & Spirit practice.

Foreword by Roger Jahnke, O.M.D.

Every year 1 out of 3 people aged 65 years and over experience a preventable fall. This is a tragedy, a monumental waste of money. Something must be done to curb this epidemic. The amazing truth is that it is actually pretty easy for people to retain their wellbeing and balance to prevent such falls.

Roxanne's very comprehensive book outlines simple steps that give each person a choice, do I change and take more responsibility for my health or do I expect health care professionals to make these choices for me? The former choice is the one of a proactive, enthusiastic, self-reliant member both family and society. The latter, the victim view, is frankly a problem to families and the society.

I have known Roxanne Reynolds for many years. Her guidelines for fall prevention are actually a recipe for life long wellbeing. She cares deeply for our elders and is committed to playing her part - a major part -- in helping to stop falls. Roxanne has attended many of the trainings at the Institute of Integral Qigong and Tai Chi (IIQTC) and she is a certified Tai Chi Easy Practice Leader and Teacher of Mind-Body

Practice. Over the years I have come to know Roxanne, her character and things that she cares deeply about. She frequently expresses her love of those from older generations and her commitment to foster robust health and wellbeing for all populations, especially including our elders.

Over her many years of teaching T'ai Chi to seniors and specialized exercise to people with movement disorders, Roxanne has sadly seen first hand what can happen after one falls. Being a woman of action, these falls inspired her to write this book which brings striking awareness to the magnitude of falls so prevalent today. In <u>A Senior's Guide To Fall Prevention and Healthy Living</u> Roxanne outlines simple strategies to fall prevention - what might better be called balance enhancement. It is thrilling that balanced living creates the reduction of the waste of funds and human energy. I enthusiastically recommend this book to citizens of all ages regarding prevention of distress and sickness-and especially in preventing falls.

Preface

Over the past 10 years I have had the pleasure of working with and learning from the elders in our society, especially those afflicted with Parkinson's disease. In my work I have discovered just how many people have balance concerns and fall on a regular basis. My experience teaching t'ai chi, qigong and specialized exercise classes to the seniors has given me great insight into their quiet suffering. I found a great lack of information and study regarding fall prevention among this population.

My dear grandmother, Anna, broke both of her hips, one when she was 79 and the other when she was 84. She was never the same and lived the last 5 years of her life in a nursing home with 24 hour care.

I have seen the results of falls {the black eyes, bruising, fractured and broken hips, legs, and sometimes even death}. I have visited my friends in hospitals, rehab and long term care facilities. Most of us don't think we will ever fall, because if we did, we would take every possible precaution and preventative action.

Being proactive and taking responsibility starts with ourselves and we must take steps to curb this epidemic.

Falls are the leading cause of non fatal injuries in the United States.

I decided to create a simple effective guide to help empower seniors and those with debilitating health issues.

The information contained in this book is simple, straight forward, yet highly effective, and can be used on a daily basis as a guide to help reduce the staggering number of accidents that threaten our health and longevity. It is with much love and devotion to the elderly, and a special inclusion to my friends with Parkinson's, that I dedicate this book.

Acknowledgements

First and foremost I would like to thank my students, past and present, because without them the need for this book would have never been realized.

My heart is filled with gratitude to all who helped make this book a reality. To Kim Saxon and Sarah Sperber, thanks for your encouragement on this project and for reading the book over. Thanks to Dianne O'Brien and Nancy Hillrich for your excellent editing skills and Linda Bettcher for proof reading and always brightening my day. Very special thanks to my long time friend Jamie Snyder, for providing guidance, spiritually, professionally, financially and supporting my vision.

Much adoration and love to my parents for always encouraging me in every way and a special thank you to my mother who makes me laugh from the belly and who symbolizes real love. I am so fortunate to have you mom.

Much love and appreciation to you all!

Fall Statistics

According to the National Center for Health Statistics, there were 34 million people over the age of 65 in 1997, and that will double to nearly 70 million by 2030.

Did you know?

- Every year more than 11 million senior citizens fall; that's one out of three people age 65 years and older
- According to the Centers for Disease Control, CDC, and Prevention, in 2003 more than 1.8 million people 65 and older were treated in emergency room departments for fall-related injuries. Of these, more than 421,000 were hospitalized
- In 2009 2.2 million non fatal fall injuries among older adults were treated in emergency departments and more than 581,000 of these patients were hospitalized; CDC 2010
- Falls are the most common cause of injury and the 6th leading cause of death for seniors

- In 2005, 15,800 people 65 years and older died from injuries related to unintentional falls; CDC 2008
- In 2007 over 18,000 older adults died from unintentional falls
- From 1970 to 1995, the age-adjusted incidence of falling has increased over 124%
- In 1970 there were 5,622 falls, which are 494 per 100,000 people
- In 1995 there were 21,574 falls, which are 1,398 per 100,000 people

Annually $20.2 billion is spent for the treatment of fall related injuries. Most of that money is spent for the treatment of hip fractures, which averages $35,000 per patient. Falls among older adults cause 90% of broken hips. According to the Journal of the American Medical Association JAMA (July 25, 2007 edition) more than 30,000 hip fractures occur every year. Hip fractures are one of the main reasons why people end up in nursing homes. 30% of people who break a hip die within 1 year. In 2003, about 72% of older adults admitted to the hospital for hip fractures were women; CDC 2005. Of the older adults who are discharged for fall-related hip fractures, about half or 53% will experience another fall within 6 months.

Recent studies have shown that falls are the most common cause of traumatic brain injuries and these injuries account for 46% of fatal falls among older adults.

There are many factors as to how and why people, mainly seniors, lose their balance. The more risk factors a person has, the greater the likelihood that they will fall. Many of these risk factors are preventable. A lack of knowledge leads to a lack of preventative action, which can result in falls.

This book was published to inform you, the consumer, of ways to distinguish weaknesses and to encourage action be taken so that YOU do not become a statistic. No one expects to fall, as the following story demonstrates.

Seat Belts – Other People Maybe, Not Him

By Dan Verver

Watching my parents grow older, (we live in the same city), is like watching the sun set in slow motion. One of the things I would hear about when I would visit was my dad's difficulty not so much in falling asleep as in staying asleep. So his sleep was getting spread around, some at night, and some during the day. He also had problems with hearing and walking. I don't know if it was a matter of pride or refusing to acknowledge the fact that he was getting older, but he hated using a cane and disliked using his walker even more. He would use them if he went out, probably because we would tell him, "If you don't take it with you, you're not going." But at home, he wouldn't touch them. His walking had deteriorated from the point of one foot in front of the other to one heel in front of the other. We would tell him he could lose his balance and fall and he would say that wasn't going to happen. My brother would ask him how he knew that. My brother would ask him to name one person that fell who knew it was going to happen before it did. Seat belts. Why do we wear seat belts when we drive somewhere? Because we are going to get in an accident or because the possibility exists so we take the necessary precaution and buckle up. Did dad see the correlation? Not really. He refused to acknowledge the possibility that he could fall, other people maybe but not him.

My dad died in August of 2008. He was found in the morning on the bathroom floor. From what we can surmise, he had been sitting up, reading, during the night, got up and went into the bathroom. For whatever reason, it appears he lost his balance, and in falling, hit his head on one of the towel bars and landed face down on the floor. He managed to roll over onto his back and that's how he was found. We're guessing that in the struggle to get back up his heart gave out. We won't ever know. The tragedy in all of this is that if he had used his cane or his walker, the possibility exists that he wouldn't have fallen, and might not have died.

We don't put seat belts on because we are going to get into an accident; we put them on to increase our chances for survival. Take it from me; you don't have to be old to fall down. Everybody falls down at one time or another. Some of us haven't fallen since we were learning how to walk, and if we realize that a fall can still happen, we can keep it that way.

Chapter 1

Is Your Home Safe?

Great tips on providing a safer home. We spend most of our time at home and this is where most falls take place.

"May your troubles be less, your blessings be more and nothing but happiness come through your door."
~ Anonymous

Your Home

Is Your Home Safe? - The home is a place of comfort, security and safety for everyday living. Unfortunately, one-third of all falls in the elderly involve environmental hazards in the home. The most common hazard for falls is tripping over objects on the floor. Other factors include poor lighting, loose rugs, lack of grab bars and unsteady furniture.

Don't Take Risks!

Sometimes older adults ignore their changing physical abilities and attempt to do too much. Examples are clearing snow and ice off the walkway, pruning trees, using ladders or unsteady stools, walking without mobility aid when one is needed or not using hand rails and grab bars.

Fifty-five percent of all falls take place inside the home. There are close to 200,000 accidents in the bathroom each year. That's 70% of all home accidents. A little bit of time spent installing safety precautions in your bathroom, living area, bedroom, and kitchen can ensure years of accident free living.

Linda's Story

On July 31, 2010 I stumbled over the bathroom scale and fractured my left hip in four places. It all began with my Siamese cat, also known as Mighty Hunter, jumping from towel racks to shelves to the night light in his efforts to corner a small moth. My daughter joined the activity trying to catch the cat before he knocked bath powder jars on the floor. I was fascinated by the whole crazy circus act, and I backed up without paying attention to what was behind me. I tripped over the scale, landed on the floor and knew instantly I would not be able to walk again anytime soon.

The next day, I opened my eyes in the hospital recovery room after several hours of surgery. Due to osteoporosis, my pelvis was too fragile to support a total hip replacement, so the surgeons planted pieces of metal in four different incisions. This resulted in my left leg becoming 1 1/4" shorter than the right leg, but, what the heck? At least, I still had two functioning legs, and after a couple of months, I was able to navigate without walkers or canes. I had wonderful physical therapists, and, yes I worked darn hard!

My story is an example of what can happen when the brain loses its focus and pays attention to what's going on elsewhere. Since that time, I have been practicing Roxanne's good advice to "live in the now." When I'm walking anywhere or reaching into cabinets or hurrying to answer the phone, I work hard at trying to stay involved in what I'm doing at the moment. If my brain wants to multi-task, I wait until I am seated firmly in a chair….and not chasing the cat or running downstairs.

Please think about the suggestions Roxanne is giving you in this book. ONE OF THEM COULD SAVE YOUR LIFE.

Outside the Home

- Clear all pathways around the home of clutter and use nonslip surfaces
- Fill holes in concrete and be sure the surface is even
- Keep tools and yard equipment securely stored
- You must have adequate lighting with bright porch lights, consider installing security lighting
- Are the steps in good repair with step edges marked? Paint the doorsill a different color than the floor to avoid tripping
- Install handrails on stairs and steps
- Mix sand and paint for a rough non-slip surface on basement or outdoor steps

Inside the Home

- Remove clutter, throw rugs (or use nonslip backing and carpet tape) and keep electric, appliance and telephone cords out of walkways, not under rugs
- Remove newspapers and debris from all pathways and arrange furniture to ensure clear passage
- Keep easy access to light switches and use frosted light bulbs of at least 60 watts, or use a lamp shade to help prevent glare. Use motion sensing night lights
- If you have stairs, use reflective tape on the steps to help you see, especially at night. And be sure the stairs are slip-resistant and have handrails. In 1990, nearly 1 million people required hospital room treatment from falls on steps and stairs
- Remove your reading glasses before using the stairs
- Use sturdy chairs with straight backs, firm seats and arm rests. Avoid chairs and sofas that are so low they are difficult to get out of
- Avoid step ladders, but if you must use one, make sure it has a high handle for support and that stool treads are slip resistant and in good

condition. In British Columbia steps and stairs
are among the most frequent sites of falls and the
leading category for mortality from falls

In the Bedroom

- Keep all pathways from the bed to the bathroom clear and use a night light(s)
- The mattress on the bed should be firm enough to support a seated person without sagging, and also be approximately 18" from the top of mattress to the floor
- Get out of bed slowly; give yourself time to adjust to an upright position. This is a great time to stretch and limber your body
- If you have trouble getting out of bed switch to high thread count sheets, this can make it easier
- Have a night stand near the bed with an easily accessible lamp or light switch, phone, emergency phone numbers, whistle and a flashlight for emergencies
- Wear a short robe {to prevent tripping} and well fitted slippers
- Have a firm chair, with arms, to sit and dress
- Use motion sensing night lights along walking pathways

In the Bathroom

- Be sure the door is wide enough to move through easily, with or without an assistive device (cane, walker, and wheelchair). Door can be removed for easier access
- Ensure the threshold is low enough to avoid tripping, and that the flooring has a non-slip surface
- Use an elevated toilet seat with grab bars within reach
- In the shower, use a bath chair and a hand held shower. Install grab bars, plus place nonskid strips on shower floor and in the bathtub
- Be sure outlets are ground fault circuit interrupters (GFCI) to protect against electric shock in the bathroom
- Check water temperature before entering the bath or shower
- Be sure you have good lighting, even lighting without glare. Use a regular nightlight or motion sensing nightlight
- Never shower alone if you are on strong medication or frail

- Walk-in bathtubs offer seniors the chance to bathe in safety and the comfort of getting to soak in a tub. Walk-in tubs work by providing a door to step into the bathtub as opposed to stepping over the tub edge
- Many find that keeping a red light on in darkened rooms (like the hallway or bathroom) makes it easier to see than using a "regular" night light. Red light produces fewer glares than a regular incandescent bulb
- Install a liquid soap dispenser on the bathtub shower wall
- Make sure floor rugs are secured with non-slip backing

Warning: Everyday one person dies from using a shower/bathtub in the United States.

In the Kitchen

- A well organized kitchen will make cooking and cleaning easier, more enjoyable and safer
- Avoid placing objects out of reach. You are more likely to fall when climbing and reaching high places
- If you need to use a step ladder, (which can be very dangerous) be sure it has a high handle for support and the stool treads are slip- resistant and in good condition
- Clean up spills right away to avoid slipping and falling
- Use lightweight pots and pans and have pot holders and mitts within reach
- Keep pet dishes away from walking area
- Dishes and food should be stored on lower shelves for easy access
- Again, be sure lighting is good, especially around and over the sink, stove and counter tops
- Flooring should be nonslip
- Use a whistling tea pot, food timers and brightly colored tape on OFF indicators

- Be sure tables and chairs are strong and secure enough to provide support when leaning, standing or sitting

Where are Your Pets?

Do you have pets? Know where your pet is before getting up from a chair or walking into your home. Place a bell or something you can hear on its collar, to alert you to the pets location. Also, keep your pets water and food dishes out of the way.

The Centers for Disease Control found cats and dogs often trip their owners, accounting for more than 80,000 falls a year in the U.S. Nearly 90% of the pet related falls were blamed on dogs. Women were more than twice as likely to be injured as men.[1]

Find the right pet. Older, calmer pets are less likely to jump and get tangled in between your legs. Train your dog. This will be time and money well spent.

Chapter 2

Body & Health

Tips and ideas on ways to improve your physical and mental health. Our energy comes from getting enough rest, having a healthy mindset, drinking clean water, eating fresh foods and exercise.

"Old age is not determined by the number of years you have lived, but by the ideals you hold, and the enthusiasm of your soul. Youth's beauty is replaced by age's grace"

~ Anonymous

Do You Have Optimal Health?

Our energy tends to decrease as we age, but we can help maintain good health and vitality by exercising and eating a healthy diet. Studies of the oldest inhabitants on this planet reveal they lived on a simple diet of fresh, locally grown foods, lightly cooked.

Did you know only 25% of Americans get the recommended daily servings of fruits and vegetables that protect against disease? Eat life-enhancing foods and drink enough water. Water plays a vital role in maintaining balance in the body.

Former US Surgeon General Koop warned Americans in a landmark 1988 report on nutrition and health that diet-related diseases account for 68% of deaths![1]

Please take responsibility for your own health and make the necessary changes to enhance your health physically and mentally. No one can do this for you.

Our Bodies Are Our Gardens
Our Wills Are Our Gardeners"
William Sharkespeare

Vitamin D for Defense

Studies indicate that inadequate levels of vitamin D are associated with chronic diseases like high blood pressure, tuberculosis, cancer, periodontal (gum) disease, MS, chronic pain, depression, schizophrenia, SAD (seasonal affective disorder), peripheral artery disease and various autoimmune diseases. "Vitamin D has a global effect on many systems", said Bruce Hollis,[2] a professor of pediatrics & biochemistry and molecular biology at the Medical University of South Carolina. Also affected are muscle strength and increased risk of falling. Colorectal, prostate, breast and other major cancers all become more common in the absence of sufficient vitamin D. The maximum production by your body with full sun exposure on a naked body is about 10,000 IU per day. The RDA is 400 IU a day but those recommendations were last updated in 1997 and were aimed mostly at preventing bone diseases, such as rickets in children and osteoporosis in the elderly.

Since then, studies have shown that vitamin D offers a host of health benefits including a lower risk of falls. A five month study done in a nursing home involved its 124 nursing home residents:

- Group 1 received 800 IU of vitamin D a day
- Group 2 received 600 IU of vitamin D a day

- Group 3 received 400 IU of vitamin D a day
- Group 4 received 200 IU of vitamin D a day
- Group 5 were given a sugar pill

The researchers found that the residents getting 800 IU of vitamin D daily fell far less than did residents getting lower amounts of vitamin D or no D. Those getting 800 IU of the vitamin were 72% less likely to fall. Two-thirds of nursing home residents were already getting a multivitamin with 400 IU of vitamin D so somewhere between 800-1200 IU per day was required to prevent falls in nursing home residents. [3] (From The Journal of the American Geriatrics Society).

If you think your vitamin D levels are low or you would like to know your vitamin D levels, have a blood test and find out. Forty percent of Americans (especially women) are deficient in vitamin D. Twenty minutes a day of early morning sunshine makes a real difference to your body's vitamin D levels, especially if you are at risk for osteoporosis.

You can get vitamin D from the following foods: raw sunflower seeds, wheat germ, sweet potatoes, alfalfa, natural vegetable oils, cod liver oil, salmon, herring, yogurt, cheese, butter, tuna, eggs and liver.

Diet – Eat Nutritious Foods

"Let food be thy medicine and medicine be thy food."
Hippocrates, the Father of Medicine (460-377 B.C.)

Eat nutritious meals - you are what you eat. Your diet is the most powerful weapon you have to maintain your health. A sensible lifestyle, with healthy food, regular moderate exercise, a positive attitude and restful sleep are still the best medicine for many health conditions.

Nature has provided the human body with an amazing immune system, designed to heal itself. Too often, when illness strikes, we expect health care professionals to cure us. What we fail to understand is that the cure comes from within. Your body is designed as a self-healing system and all people should take an active role in the maintenance of their health and in the treatments of their disorders, with the guidance of a health care professional.

As we age, our ability to produce and absorb nutrients diminishes. Also, any illness or disease will increase our nutritional needs. Medications can interfere with nutrient absorption and deplete the body's nutritional stores. These issues can be improved through nutritional supplementation.

Benefits of a healthy diet include:
- Increased mental acuteness

- Resistance to illness and disease
- Higher energy levels
- A much better immune system and faster recuperation times
- Better management of chronic health problems

Eat organic whenever possible. Foods labeled organic cannot be treated with chemical fertilizers, pesticides or herbicides. If you do not buy organic be sure to wash your fruits and vegetables with a produce wash, available at most health food stores. This will help remove chemical sprays, waxes and soils. Also, buy seasonal from local farmers and eat a wide variety of vegetables and fruits.

The more fruits and vegetables you eat, the more nutrition you get, lowering your risk of disease. It's best to consume fruits and vegetables in their raw state and when fresh because fresher veggies and fruits contain more vitamins and enzymes than those that have been cooked or stored for a long time. If you like cooked veggies then lightly steam or use a wok.

Eat lean meats and poultry and consider getting some of your protein from plant sources: whole grains like quinoa, beans, peas, nuts, seeds, soy foods {like tofu and soybeans}, leafy vegetables, collard greens, kale, broccoli, cabbage and cauliflower. Super foods like blue green algae, sea greens and chlorella are also good sources of protein, as well as, nutritional yeast, sprouts and seeds like almonds, sunflower and pumpkin. It is best to eat nuts and seeds raw for digestibility. If you have trouble digesting nuts, fruits and vegetables, try digestive enzymes, available at health food stores.

Yogurt is a good source of protein. Yogurt contains bacteria responsible for maintaining good flora in the digestive tract.

Buy yogurt without added sugar or flavoring. Sugar feeds unwanted bacteria.

Eat complex carbohydrates and benefit from a constant flow of energy. In contrast, simple carbohydrates give you a short lived rush. Refined carbohydrates {sugar} can lead to many disorders. You can find complex carbohydrates in fresh fruits and vegetables, beans and natural whole grains.

Limit the use of salt and sodium. Check out sea greens. Sea greens help re-mineralize your body. They are powerful healers and are the most nutritionally dense plants on the planet. Crush, chop or crumble any mix of dry sea greens and add to soups, rice, salads or casseroles. Sea greens include kelp, wakame, dulse nori and kombu. Excellent! Available in most health food stores.

Stay away from Trans-Fatty acids, foods like margarine and fried foods. Trans Fats are primarily found in processed baked goods and fried foods. How do you know whether foods contain trans fat? Look for the words "partially hydrogenated" vegetable oil. That's another name for trans fat. Read labels carefully.

Eat more good fats {omega 3 fats} like wild caught salmon or tilapia. Add walnuts, pumpkin seeds, or their oil to your salad or pasta. Also add flaxseeds or flaxseed oil and green vegetables, grains and omega 3 enriched eggs, available at health food stores.

Ideally a good rule of thumb is to eat the main meal at breakfast or lunch with a light meal during early evening.

Recipes for Cleaning Fruits/Vegetables

Mix vinegar and water in equal proportions, pour in spray bottle and use to clean produce. Or mix 1 TBSP lemon juice, 2 TBSP baking soda and 1 cup of water, pour in spray bottle and use.

Drink Good Quality Water

Most of our tap water is chlorinated and or fluoridated. Drink quality water whenever possible: bottled, distilled or install a purification system. Reasons to drink quality water include:

- Keeps the brain sharp
- Helps eliminate toxins in the blood stream
- Cleans the kidneys
- Great for weight loss by suppressing the appetite
- Helps you feel full and also helps the body metabolize stored fat

Experts in health, Paul C Bragg N.D. PhD and Patricia Bragg N.D. PhD, recommend daily consumption of 8-10 glasses of pure distilled water. Distilled water has no inorganic minerals to deposit on the walls of the arteries and other vessels of the body.

Angina, allergies, asthma, back and joint pains, migraines, stomach pains and arthritis may all be symptoms of severe dehydration-which can easily be helped by drinking 8 to 10 glasses of quality drinking water daily! Start increasing your water intake today.

Hip fracture rates are much higher in people living in fluoridated communities. [4]

Hip Fractures and Fluoridation in Utah's Elderly Population, a study by C. Danielson et al [Journal of the

American Medical Association, August 12, 1992, 268:746-8], compared the incidence of femoral neck fractures in a community with long-standing water fluoridation (to 1 ppm) with the incidence in two communities without water fluoridation (less than 0.3 ppm). The findings of this report support other epidemiologic studies suggesting that fluoride increases the risk of hip fracture.

Dehydration Avoidance

Studies show that dehydration is one of the top ten causes of hospital stays among the elderly. Fifty percent of all dehydrated seniors die within one year. (Warren et al. 1994)

Common Symptoms of Dehydration

- Headaches, usually with <u>dizziness</u> & fatigue
- Irritability, restlessness, difficulty sleeping
- Dry skin, no appetite, constipation
- Dull backache
- Weight gain - swollen hands and feet (from water retention)
- Bloating, urinating less (urine is dark color, should be light yellow color, like pale straw)

Causes of Dehydration may include

- Inability to drink fluids
- Diarrhea
- Vomiting
- Sweating
- Diabetes and burns

Many seniors fear incontinence so they drink less. According to Dr. Linda Page Ph.D., people with incontinence can help this condition by supplementing their diet with

3,000 mg vitamin C daily. Also, B12 deficiency is linked to incontinence in the elderly. Dr. Page recommends a high potency sublingual B-12, up to 2500-10,000 mcg. Kegel exercises also help with incontinence.

Dehydration can cause

- Chronic constipation
- Urinary tract infections
- Vascular problems like hemorrhoids and varicose veins
- Kidney stones
- Plus a contributing factor to arthritis

Normal activities require about 3 quarts of replacement water a day. Strenuous activity, living in a hot climate or a high salt diet increases this requirement. Use micro-clustered water to re-hydrate fast. Micro-clustered water also enhances absorption of supplements and food nutrients. One of the most popular brands of micro-clustered water is the PENTA brand, which can be purchased at better health food stores.

Kegel Exercise

To get started you need to find the pelvic muscles. To help find the right muscles try to stop the flow of urine while you're going to the bathroom. If that worked you have found the correct muscles.

- Sit down
- Contract your pelvic muscles
- Hold for 3 seconds and then relax for 3 seconds

- Repeat 10-15 times
- Relax & Breathe

Practice the exercise daily and within 8-12 weeks you should have less leakage.

Magnesium

Magnesium intake may be linked to higher bone density. Studies [12] show that getting key bone-building nutrients (such as calcium, vitamin D and magnesium) plus regular weight bearing exercise may help lower your risk of fractures. Fifty percent of white women 80 years old and older have osteoporosis. These women also have the highest risk of suffering a hip fracture at 16%. In comparison, black women and white men run a 6% risk, and black men a 3% risk. As we age our bone density diminishes. (Low bone density = osteoporosis.) When this happens, the risk of bone fractures increase. The most feared is a hip fracture. 30% of people who suffer from a hip fracture die within one year and 53% will fall again within 6 months.

Ask your doctor if you should get a bone density test. The dual x-ray densitometry machine determines the density of bones in the hip, spine and wrist.

The RDA {Recommended Daily Allowance} of magnesium for women is 420 mg per day and for men 320 mg per day. If you take supplements use forms of calcium or magnesium that are highly absorbable like citrate or aspartates.

Good sources of magnesium—Cooked or raw dark leafy greens, kelp, nuts, seeds, legumes, poultry, soy beans, kale, endive, chard, beet tops, celery, figs, apples, brown rice, sunflower and sesame seeds.

Good sources of calcium—Dark leafy greens, endive, cabbage, kale, dandelion greens, brussel sprouts, broccoli, tofu, molasses, shellfish, sesame seeds and sea greens are especially good.

Increase Bone Density

Bone loss increases your susceptibility to falls and fractures. Experts from the National Osteoporosis Foundation predict over 40 million Americans will suffer from Osteoporosis by the year 2015. Since people with osteoporosis cannot feel their bones getting weaker, they do not know they have osteoporosis until they break a bone. People with osteoporosis most often break a bone in the hip, spine or wrist. But they can also break other bones, sometimes from simple actions such as sneezing or hugging.

You are never too young or too old to protect your bones. Take action now!

A major cause of osteoporosis is an inadequate intake of calcium over a period of years. Other causes are inability to absorb sufficient calcium through the intestines, calcium-phosphorus imbalance, lack of exercise, or lack of certain hormones. Consider a high quality plant mineral supplement that includes calcium, B vitamins, magnesium, silica, boron and manganese for best absorption. The Institute of Medicine recommends 1,000 mg of calcium daily for women between the ages of 19 and 50, 1200 mg after age 50.

A twelve year study of 78,000[10] women showed that a high consumption of milk and other dairy foods did not reduce bone breaks or osteoporosis. In fact, the study showed instead that a hip fracture was 1.45 times higher in women who drank 2 or more glasses of milk a day compared to those who drank one glass or less per week. More studies show that high dairy product intake was significantly associated with hip fractures.[11] Good dairy substitutes include, kefir, {350mg of calcium per cup}, soy milk, rice milk and almond milk.

Too much animal protein actually contributes to osteoporosis, heart disease and cancers, like renal cancer and lymph sarcoma, through loss of critical minerals.[5] Research shows that eating lots of high protein animal foods may cause your body to extract calcium from your blood and excrete it.

Regular exercise and overall good nutrition stressing fresh, mineral rich vegetables like broccoli, kale, spinach and collard greens are probably better ways of dealing with osteoporosis than taking huge amounts of calcium supplements. Beneficial mineral rich herbs include kelp, dulse, burdock, oat straw and dandelion. An 8 ounce glass of fresh carrot juice has 400 mg of bio-available calcium.

Caffeine and Bone Health—Excessive caffeine causes calcium depletion, which increases the risk of osteoporosis. If you have osteoporosis, limit the amount of caffeine you consume for optimum mineral assimilation.

Sea Greens and Bone Health—Sea greens are loaded with body building minerals like calcium, iron, iodine and potassium. Magnesium, which is essential for calcium absorption, is rich in sea greens. Magnesium stimulates production of calcitonin, the hormone which increases calcium in the bones. Sea greens are a good source of vitamin D, also vital for calcium absorption, bone health and muscle function. Sea plants include kelp, kombu, hijiki, nori, arame, sea palm, bladderwrack, wakame, dulse and irish moss.

Fractures from osteoporosis result in more deaths in women than ovarian and breast cancer combined (Br MedJ96; 312:570-572).

In a clinical study[6] researchers found that vibration devices have the potential to play a significant part in maintaining bone health in post menopausal women. See page on Whole Body Vibration for more information.

Because of the possibility of interactions with prescription medications, dietary supplements should be taken only under the supervision of a knowledgeable health care provider.

Rest

Get enough rest - Get enough rest to keep your immune system strong. Sleep is necessary in order for the nervous system to work properly. With too little sleep we are left drowsy and unable to concentrate. This also leads to impaired memory and physical performance.

Drugs - Prescription and non prescription drugs can cause sleep problems. Common prescription drugs that can affect sleep are high blood pressure medication, diet pills, inhaled respiratory medications, some antidepressants and steroids, including prednisone.

Alcohol disrupts sleep patterns by preventing you from getting deep sleep and REM sleep because alcohol keeps you in the lighter stages of sleep. Sleep disruption leads to daytime fatigue and sleepiness. The elderly are especially at risk for alcohol related sleep disorders because they achieve higher levels of it in the blood and brain than do younger adults, and it can lead to unsteadiness with increased risk of falls and injuries.

Caffeine - consumed late in the day or night disrupts sleep patterns. In a 1998 study, conducted in Australia, it showed regular caffeine users sleep longer and more soundly when caffeine is cut from their diet.

A Good Night Sleep Tips

- Progressive relaxation {following page}
- A warm bath with lavender
- Avoid heavy meals late in the evening
- No electrical appliance near you while in bed
- Chamomile or passion flower tea before bed
- Go to bed at the same time every night
- Exercise during the day 20-30 minutes
- Avoid caffeine, alcohol, or other stimulants
- Valerian: soothes nerves and eases muscle tension. A good sedative for insomnia. In a double blind study involving 128 subjects it was shown that an aqueous extract of valerian root improved the subjective ratings for sleep quality and sleep latency(the time required to go to sleep), but left no "hangover" the next morning[7]
- Tryptophan administered at a dose of 1 to 3 grams has been shown to reduce the time required to go to sleep as well as to decrease awakenings in numerous double-blind clinical studies[8] Wyatt R, Engelman K, Kupffer D, etal,; Effects of L-tryptophan (a natural sedative) on human sleep. Lancet ii;842-846,1970

Because of the possibility of interactions with prescription medications and over the counter medications, dietary supplements should be taken only under the supervision of a knowledgeable health care provider.

Progressive Relaxation (in 5 minutes)

Focus and consciously relax each part of your body, from the feet all the way up to your head. Your breath should be full and relaxed. It is particularly easy to do in bed before sleep.

- Lie down, close your eyes and take 10 slow deep breaths
- Focus on your right leg. Inhale deeply and lift the leg slightly tensing the foot and leg. Tense up tighter. Exhale and let the leg drop gently. Roll the leg from side to side and relax. Repeat on the left leg
- Focus on your thighs and buttocks. Inhale, contract your buttocks, pelvic muscles and the thighs. Tighten until the end of the breath and then release and exhale
- Focus on your right arm. Inhale, raise and tense your right arm and make your hand into a fist. Tense up and hold. Exhale and drop the arm. Roll the right arm from side to side. Inhale and repeat with the left arm
- Bring the shoulder blades together in back as you inhale. Squeeze and release, exhale
- Bring your shoulders up to your ears as you inhale. Hold them for a few seconds and as you exhale bring the shoulders down Repeat 3-4 times

- Inhale, tighten the facial muscles, as if you have just bitten into a lemon or something sour and squeeze tightly. Exhale and release tension
- Roll your head from side to side gently and continue to take deep relaxed breaths to go deeper and deeper into relaxation

Mental Alertness

Movement is crucial to brain health. Exercise increases oxygen and blood supply to the brain, making it a key brain nutrient. Studies show that physically active seniors demonstrated much better thinking and memory skills than those living sedentary lifestyles. A study at the Group Cooperative in Seattle, Washington tracked older adults for 6 years and found that regular exercise such as walking the equivalent of at least 90 minutes per week at 21-30 minute mile pace was associated with improved cognitive performance.

- Deep breathing is important as the brain requires 3 times more oxygen than the rest of the body. Oxygen starvation is caused by shallow breathing, sedentary habits and lack of exercise and fresh air. With deep breathing your brain becomes more alert and your nervous system functions better. Deep breathing stimulates your brain cells and promotes new brain cell growth. Take in a slow deep relaxed breath right now
- Drink plenty of water for brain health. An Italian study shows that even 2% loss of body fluid affects short term memory
- Get plenty of rest. Even a few hours of sleep loss causes memory problems

- A deficiency of B-vitamins causes vascular cognitive impairment, according to a new study. [9] Researchers at the Jean Mayer USDA Human Nutrition Research Center on Aging at Tufts University used an experimental model to examine the metabolic, cognitive, and micro vascular effects of dietary B-vitamin deficiency. For more brain power consider taking a B complex supplement

- Eat Right. Good nutrition is crucial for staying mentally and physically fit. Scientists at the Department of Agriculture's Human Nutrition Research Center on Aging in Boston report that daily requirements for vitamins B-6, B-12, C,D and E escalate with age, along with the need for calcium, beta carotene and folic acid. Quality food is powerful medicine. Stay away from unnecessary sources of sugar {like soda and other sweetened beverages}. Eliminate processed and refined foods, like white bread, white rice and pasta. Instead switch to whole grains, an excellent source of B vitamins, and eat plenty of fruits and vegetables rich in vitamins and powerful antioxidants

- Are you malnourished in vitamins and minerals that support mental functions? Eat plenty of high antioxidant foods, like raisins, blueberries, blackberries, raspberries, strawberries, kale and spinach

- Feed your brain with omega-3 fats by eating omega enriched eggs, cold water fish like {halibut, mackerel, salmon, trout, and tuna}, flaxseed, walnuts and green vegetables
- Stay away from-Trans Fatty Acids by not buying products that have "partially hydrogenated vegetable oil" or "partially hydrogenated vegetable shortening". This includes processed, refined foods like commercial bread, crackers, cookies, and snack foods. Read the labels carefully. Stay away from deep fried foods, instead bake, sauté, steam or grill

According to Dr. Larry M. C. Cleary, author of The Brain Trust Program, stay away from trans fats and high fructose corn syrup, as they both disrupt and damage brain cells. Read labels carefully on the food you buy.

The Better Brain Book authors David Perlmutter, M.D., FACN and Carol Colman recommend four tests that can help determine potential brain and neurological problems. These tests are: The Lipid Peroxide Test, Homocysteine Check, The ApoE4 GENOTYPE The "Alzheimer's Gene" and the C-Reactive Protein test. Check with your health care provider to see which of these tests are covered by your insurance.

Brain boosting ideas

- Work or volunteer
- Play games and do crossword puzzles
- Find a walking partner
- Your brain is like a muscle, use it or lose it

- Be a life long learner by attending a Community College
- Socialize or live with someone. Having daily interactions and conversations is good for your health

Limit Alcohol

Limit alcohol intake. Alcohol may potentially increase the risk of falls in the elderly population. Alcohol can increase the sedative and negative neuromuscular side effects of many medications.

Chronic alcohol consumption is one of the strongest predictors of high blood pressure. It also can harm the liver, brain and heart. Alcohol impairs sleep by causing the release of adrenaline, and impairs the transport of the amino acid tryptophan into the brain, where it is converted to serotonin, a natural sleep promoting substance.

Chapter 3

Care Of Your Feet

Covers one of the most neglected parts of the body - our feet, which are most often abused from improper footwear and poor circulation.

"The human foot is a masterpiece of engineering and a work of art."
~ Leonardo da Vinci

Care of Your Feet

Balance starts here. The most common cause of foot problems is ill-fitting shoes. Women have four times as many foot problems as men, mainly because women wear high heels. Frequent wearing of high heels has been related to the gradual buildup of heel spurs. Incorrect shoe length has been significantly associated with ulceration of the foot and with pain. Overly narrow footwear has been strongly associated with the presence of corns on the toes.

There are 26 bones in each foot-more than any other part of the body. It is vital that enough blood reaches the feet in the required quantities, or toxins will collect in the cell structures of the feet. Tight shoes, more than any other article of clothing, do more to disturb the circulation of blood to the feet. Only wear comfortable, well-fitted shoes that don't bind or inhibit the circulation of blood to the feet.

Leg and Feet Vibrating Exercise

Stand tall, feet about 8-10 inches apart and arms at sides. Put all your weight on your left foot and raise your right foot off the ground 6-8 inches. Make short stretching kicks in a forward direction. (It may be a good idea to hold onto a chair or sit if unsteady.) You should feel vibration from the hips to the toes. Now repeat the same on the other side. Start with 10 kicks on each foot and increase the amount every day until you can kick up to 30 times or more with each foot. This will promote great circulation to hips, thighs, calves and feet.

Suggestions to help with flexibility and circulation of your feet:

- Spend a few minutes a day spreading your toes apart or use toe combs {used when applying toe nail polish}.
- Place the balls of the feet on a hard cover book or piece of wood that is about 1¼ inches thick and then place the heels of your feet on the floor. Hold 30 seconds-do not bounce.
- Walk barefoot or roll your feet on wooden foot rollers.
- Walk on a cobblestone mat
- Self-massage
- Pedicure and foot massage
- Reflexology

Shoes

Shoes-non-skid, non-friction soles are best. A study done through interviews with older adults who fell while hospitalized revealed that in 51% of the falls, poorly-fitted shoes played a role. (www.sciencedirect.com)

Look for materials that cushion feet but are rigid enough to give sufficient support. Soft leather is supple but supportive, and neoprene absorbs shock. The heel also should be as wide as the back of the shoe-not tapered-to lend stability and comfort. Try shoes without thick treads, which can stick and cause falls.

When shopping:

- Measure both feet. Don't assume that you wear the same size now that you wore five years ago; feet get larger as we age
- Be size wise - If one foot is bigger, buy the size that fits the bigger foot and add an insole, if needed, for the smaller foot
- Women who can not find wide enough athletic shoes for proper fit should shop in the men's shoe department because men's shoes are made wider
- Keep it on. Wear the shoe for at least 10 minutes in the store

- Carry your socks. Wear the same socks to try on shoes that you'll wear to walk. If you use an orthotic, bring it along
- Use a long handled shoe horn if you have trouble putting on your shoes

Inappropriate footwear:
- Loose fitting shoes or slippers
- Shoes with slippery soles
- High heel shoes
- Shoes with thick soles

Frequent changing of shoe style can increase the risk of falling.

Research[1] suggests that older people should wear appropriately fitted shoes both inside and outside the house. These studies show that walking barefoot or in socks indoors is the footwear condition associated with the greatest risk of falling. Older people should wear low heeled shoes because of the negative effects high heeled shoes have on posture, gait and balance, plus its association with increased risk of falls.

Handbags or Purses - more evidence shows that heavy awkward purses or handbags can throw off the balance in the elderly making them more prone to a fall.

Alternatives to carrying large purses or handbags:
- Wear a fanny pack around the waist or use your pockets
- Try wearing a small purse that you carry on your back, like a back pack
- Carry a smaller purse, or a small lightweight crossover bag that lays over the front

Reflexology

Reflexology or zone therapy looks at the feet and hands as a mini map of the entire body. The science of reflexology believes that all body parts have energy and that they share information. This information is shared through the body's electrical system, or nervous system and these nerve endings or reflex points can be stimulated with specific pressure using thumb, finger and hand techniques.

- Reflexology helps the body by removing crystalline deposits from reflex areas (nerve endings) of feet and hands through deep pressure massage
- Reflexology relaxes tension, normalizes gland and organ function and improves circulation
- Reflexology has the potential to ease pain in aching joints, improve mobility and help with incontinence

If you are not able to have reflexology, give self massage a try. The easiest guideline for self massage is to find the sore points and then work on them. If you can't reach your feet, use foot rollers. Foot rollers are great to revive tired feet and improve circulation around the arch and ball of the foot. Massage the hands the same way, find the sore spots and work on them.

Want restful sleep? Apply pressure to both big toes. The point on the outside of your big toe, just below the tip, corresponds with the pineal gland, which regulates the sleep hormone melatonin. Rubbing the rest of the big toe releases soothing endorphins, helping to relax.

Cobblestone Mat Walking

In this exercise method, people walk barefoot on a fixed mat that has a smooth, yet undulated cobblestone-like surface. Using the principles of reflexology, the uneven surfaces of the cobblestones stimulate "acupoints" located on the soles of the feet. Researchers are showing how cobblestone mats have produced benefits:

- Reduced blood pressure in older adults
- Promotes functional mobility and balance
- Improved overall health and well being in older adults

An article published in a recent issue of the *Journal of Aging and Physical Activity* summarizes results from a pilot study,[2] which was conducted in Portland by Oregon Research Institute scientists. Elderly participants in the study experienced considerable improvements in their ability to perform **"activities of daily living,"** increased psychosocial well-being, and significantly reduced daytime sleepiness and pain. Participants also reported **greatly improved perceptions of control over falls** and had reductions in resting diastolic blood pressure.

Cobblestone mats can be purchased from www.fitterfirst.com or www.gaiam.com

Chapter 4

Check It Out

Outline of a number of diseases and afflictions associated with falls. If you have one of these your chances of falling rises.

"You yourself, as much as anybody in the entire universe, deserve your love and affection"
Buddha

Are you at risk for a fall?

There are many contributors to falls. Generally there are several risk factors, which include but are not limited to your sex, age, hearing and vision. If you fit into any of the following categories you may be at additional risk.

- Have you fallen in the past
- On medications—how many
- Suffer from low blood pressure
- Have a fear of falling
- Improper footwear
- Parkinson's disease
- Dementia/Alzheimer's Disease
- Lack of exercise
- Low vitamin D levels
- Arthritis
- Poor balance and coordination
- Osteoporosis

If you do fall tell your family or health care provider. The cause of a fall should always be investigated to avoid another fall in the future. If you see a health care provider tell them what you were doing and how you felt before you fell. Were you dizzy, lightheaded or unsteady? Were you in your home and slipped or tripped on something? Don't wait until you fall again before you **check it out!**

If you have fallen in the past, ask yourself these questions: What was I thinking about? Was my mind focused on, the present moment, or was I thinking about something else? It is essential that you remain focused on the task at hand or present circumstance to avoid a fall.

My mother decided after a series of trips and falls that she was going to walk like a lady instead of a moving train. Her decision has helped her slow down and pay attention. And she hasn't fallen since.

Physiological Profile Assessment (PPA)

Take a PPA - Physiological profile assessment, to determine how likely it is you will fall. Balance calls upon contributions from vision, peripheral sensation, vestibular sense, muscle strength, neuromuscular control and reaction time. With age, there is a progressive loss of functioning of these systems and an increased likelihood of falls.

The PPA involves a series of simple tests of vision, peripheral sensation, muscle force, reaction time, and postural sway. From this quick and easy test you will have a better idea of the likelihood of a fall. Call your physician for an assessment.

Overcoming Fear

"Fears are nothing more than a state of mind"
Napoleon Hill

Overcome fear. Do not restrict your activity. Once a person falls, fear causes people to stop being active, making it worse and them more afraid and susceptible to another fall. Inactivity creates weakness; movement creates strength, thus improving balance.

Falls are the leading cause of injury-related death and hospitalization in people age 75 years and older (Baker and Harvey, 1985). Falls can also result in disability, restriction of activity and fear of falling, all of which reduce quality of life and independence.

Dizziness and Vertigo

Dizziness and vertigo both may be caused by infections of or injuries to the inner ear. Vertigo is a result of equilibrium disturbance, making you feel lightheaded and off balance, giving a sensation of being in a spinning room. Physical injury, such as a concussion or skull fracture, may injure the inner ear; in this type of injury, dizziness may occur long after the injury is supposedly healed. Other causes of vertigo may include the following:

- Brain tumors
- Neurological disease
- Anemia
- Blockage of the ear canal or Eustachian tube
- High or low blood pressure
- Lack of oxygen or glucose in the blood
- Psychological stress
- A deficiency of vitamin B6 or niacin may cause dizziness. Include B-vitamins in the diet this may prevent and alleviate the sensation

What May Help

See a doctor for a proper diagnosis but also consider using stress management techniques like yoga, biofeedback or meditation. Chiropractic adjustments, massage therapy, {with experience in cranial treatments} acupuncture and shiatsu are also very effective therapies.

Dizziness may be a side effect of drug medications. Check with your pharmacist. One of the easiest risk factors to change is medication use. Some types of medications, in particular drugs for depression, anxiety or psychiatric illness are associated with an increased risk of falls and hip fracture. Other factors are the number of medications a person is taking and recent changes to dosages.

Cardiovascular System

Check out your **cardiovascular system**—do you have low blood pressure? If you do, you may be at risk of a fall because some older adults have poor blood flow to the brain, which is made worse by low blood pressure. Also, the body has a tendency to lose body water as we age, which places older adults at increased risk of dehydration and this can affect blood pressure. It is absolutely vital to drink enough fluids everyday. Drink 3-4 liters of water each day.

Quit smoking! The more cigarettes smoked, the longer the period of years smoked, the greater the risk of dying from heart attack or stroke.

Exercise! Numerous studies have shown a direct relationship between physical activity and cholesterol levels. People who exercise regularly have improved circulation and better cardiovascular function. Remember long sitting and crossing your legs slows down circulation.

Something to think about! The American Heart Association says that the heart needs daily exercise and a healthy, balanced diet with ample fruits and vegetables in order to remain healthy. It has been well established that vegetarians have a much lower risk of developing heart disease. Also, vegetarians reduce their risk of high cholesterol and atherosclerosis. [6]

Most people will not follow a strict vegan diet. More importantly then is a diet high in fiber and complex carbohydrates. Remove or eliminate all refined and altered fats. Add essential dietary fatty acids with nature's richest source in flax seed oil.

Food especially good for heart health! Celery, garlic, onion, walnuts and seeds, cold water fish, fish oil, salmon and mackerel, green leafy vegetables, whole grains, legumes, broccoli and citrus fruits. To lower cholesterol, reduce animal product intake.

"Your Heart Health Is In Your Hands"
Roxanne Reynolds

Natural Supplement Considerations

Hawthorn Berry - Hawthorn's ability to dilate coronary blood vessels has been repeatedly demonstrated in experimental studies.[7] Humans and animals given hawthorn extracts have demonstrated an improvement in heart metabolism. Studies have shown hawthorn extract to be helpful in reducing angina attacks as well as lowering blood pressure and serum cholesterol levels.[11]

Calcium and Magnesium Supplements - Studies have indicated that calcium and magnesium may offer some protection against the development of high blood pressure and heart disease. [8]

Bromelain - research suggests that pineapple, more specifically bromelain, may be one of the best tools we can use to help prevent and even treat heart disease. [12]

Garlic's distinctive odor is sweet to your cardiovascular system. A team of Indian scientists found that garlic slows down lipid per oxidation, a term for the kind of blood fat rancidity linked to arterial plaque development. (Researcher Stephen Fulder, PhD, author of The Garlic Book, notes that the herb helps to lower cholesterol and triglycerides.) Garlic helps to regulate blood pressure, most likely by keeping arteries from becoming stiff and narrowed while making blood less likely to clot.

Breathe "Coronary heart disease is due to a lack of oxygen received by the heart." Dr. Dean Ornish

"Healthy breathing should be the first thing taught to a heart patient." A Dutch Study conducted by a doctor named Dixhoorn, compared two groups of heart attack patients.

The first group was taught simple diaphragmatic breathing, while the second group was given no training in breathing. The breathing group had no further heart attacks, while 7 out of 12 members of the second group had second heart attacks over the next 2 years." Gay Hendricks, Ph.D. Conscious Breathing, pg. 16

"A lack of oxygen (hypoxia) is the prime cause of 1.5 million heart attacks each year." Dr. Richard Lippman, Renowned Researcher

Meditation and Prayer Harvard cardiologist Herbert Benson conducted experiments with 30 hypertensive people who knew nothing about meditation. After he taught them how, he discovered that their blood pressure did indeed go down. The blood pressure of those people who continued daily meditating and praying went down to normal. If they stopped the practice, it began to rise again. From Healthy Heart by Paul C Bragg N.D., Ph.D. and Patricia Bragg N.D., Ph.D.

Do Daily Diaphragmatic or Abdominal Breathing: to begin straighten your spine and keep your shoulders back and relaxed. Inhale slowly and deeply through the nose filling the lower lobes of the lungs. Your abdomen will expand as the diaphragm drops down, then the upper lobes of the lungs fill expanding the chest. Exhale slowly through the nose. Repeat. Use diaphragmatic breathing to help relax when you feel tense, anxious or to ease pain.

An easy way to accustom your body to breathing naturally is to practice while you are lying down. Before you drift off to sleep at night or upon awakening in the morning, take a few moments to breathe naturally. Whether you are lying down, sitting or standing when you practice, you can feel the breath best if you place your hands over your belly button as you breathe, noticing the rise and fall of the abdomen.

Because of the possibility of interactions with prescribed medications or over the counter medications, dietary supplements should be taken only under the supervision of a knowledgeable health care provider.

Anemia

Did you know that **ANEMIA** boosts the **risk of falls** in older adults? A Dutch study done in Amsterdam with nearly 400 men and women aged 65-88 was done to determine whether anemia in older adults was more likely to cause seniors to fall. The seniors' hemoglobin levels were checked to verify those who had anemia. They were asked to keep a log for 3 years and write down every time they fell.[9] The researchers found that the older adults with anemia fell more than those seniors who did not have anemia. Also noted was the likelihood of muscle weakness in those same adults resulting in more falls.

Anemia is a decrease in red blood cells that usually shows up as tiredness, fatigue, paleness and a tendency to dizziness on standing. Although lack of iron is the most common cause, there are many other substances necessary to build red blood cells. Copper, manganese, protein, calcium, vitamin E, Vitamin C and many of the B vitamins are also important. If you decide to supplement your iron intake, consider vegetable and herbal iron sources for better absorbability.

In many cases poor nutrition is the cause of anemia. According to Linda Page PhD, anemia is often linked to low leafy intake of greens.

Good sources of **Iron foods** include:
- Almonds
- Beans
- Brown rice
- Dark greens
- Tofu
- Grapes
- Brewers yeast
- Kelp & Dulse
- Seafood
- Molasses
- Beets
- Poultry
- Eggs & yams
- Alfalfa
- Peaches
- Bananas
- Prunes
- Raisins
- Whole grain cereals
- Turnip greens
- Lentils and liver

Manganese and vitamin C foods help iron uptake:
- whole grains
- vegetables
- nuts, eggs
- pineapple, citrus,
- broccoli, cauliflower, tomatoes and peppers

Potassium foods help improve red blood cell count.

- Broccoli
- Bananas
- Sunflower seeds
- Vegetables, artichokes
- Whole grains
- Kiwi and dried fruit

Avoid iron depleting sodas, caffeine, chocolate and excess alcohol.

Physical De-Conditioning

Physical de-conditioning is the deterioration of heart and skeletal muscle related to a sedentary lifestyle, debilitating disease, or prolonged bed rest.

De-conditioning is brought on by inactivity, resulting in reduced functional capacity. Excessive fear of falling and fear of pain result in activity reduction which results in muscular decline and de-conditioning.

Tips to get you moving again—if you have poor balance or get winded easily consider a regular exercise program to get you going again. "Walking should be as good as it can be so you don't have to expend much energy just to get around," says Jessie VanSwearingen, Ph.D., P.T. Associate professor of physical therapy at the University of Pittsburgh.

Re-conditioning requires a specific treatment plan that includes walking, nutrition, turning and positioning to prevent falls and medical management.

- Use a Walker
- Walk to the beat of music
- Walk in a swimming pool. There's no danger of falling and injuring yourself in the pool
- Walk around a table after the chairs have been pushed away and lightly touch the table surface

- Rock in a rocking chair and use alternate legs to generate rocking

Seattle, WA---Vibration therapy and resistance leg exercises together prevent bone-mineral loss and wasting, known to occur with prolonged bed rest, according to new research presented at the 26th Annual Meeting of the American Society of Bone and Mineral Research. [1]

"Resistive vibration exercise, as applied here, appears to completely prevent bone loss from the tibia during prolonged bed rest," conclude the study authors, Dr. Dieter Felsenberg {Manchester University, UK} and Dr. Joern Rittweger {University Medicine Berlin, Germany}.

Parkinson's disease

Do you have Parkinson's disease? Do you lose your balance easily? Parkinson's disease (PD) is a chronic progressive neurological disorder that impairs a person's ability to move. In Parkinson's disease dopamine levels in the brain become deficient resulting in impaired balance and coordination of movement. Some beginning stage signs of PD are tremor, stiffness-rigidity, slow movement and loss of balance. The cause is unknown but environmental factors, genetic factors plus aging may play a role. It's best to see a neurologist who specializes in movement disorders. Most treatment options are medication and surgery.

What can you do if you have Parkinson's?
EXERCISE, EXERCISE, EXERCISE!!!!!

Exercise can help delay and prevent some symptoms of Parkinson's disease. A lack of exercise leads to more stiffness and slowness by reducing flexibility, strength and endurance.

Benefits of regular exercise include:
- Improved balance and coordination
- Improved joint mobility and range of motion
- Increased muscle strength and flexibility
- Posture improves
- Less muscle cramping
- Stress levels reduced
- Cardiovascular fitness

Schedule a time to exercise and mark it on your calendar; make it a habit, like brushing your teeth. Find a friend to exercise with to help keep you motivated. People with Parkinson's disease, even more than other people, should have weekly exercise classes.

Eat nutritious foods. A good rule of thumb, always clean your vegetables with a fruit and vegetable wash that removes pesticides, waxes, and chemicals. Buy organic as much as possible. Also limit your exposure to the use of toxins such as insecticides and pesticides. Read more about diet and nutrition in the section on Body and Health.

T'ai Chi. A 33-person pilot study from Washington University School of Medicine[2] in St. Louis, found that people with mild to moderately severe Parkinson's disease showed improved balance, walking ability, and overall well-being after 20 t'ai chi sessions.

Stretching is a vital part of any exercise program for someone with Parkinson's disease. Stretching exercises help promote flexibility and counteract the rigidity and stiffness of Parkinson's disease. Speak to a physical therapist or exercise specialist who is familiar with Parkinson's disease.

One recent study, focusing specifically on Parkinson's found that whole body vibration therapy help significantly in the improvement of both equilibrium and gait. [3]

In her book, <u>Healthy Living</u>, Dr. Linda Page notes that free radical damage from chemicalized foods, pesticides, and aspartame residues are especially problematic in connection to Parkinson's disease.

A research study was conducted about the Prevalence of Vitamin D insufficiency in patients with Parkinson's **PD** and

Alzheimer's disease **AD**. Participants were recruited into the study between May 1992 and March 2007. Results showed: that significantly more patients with **PD**, 55% had insufficient vitamin D than did controls, 36% or patients with **AD**, 41%. [10] It is not clear if a lack of the vitamin contributes to the development or progression of the neurological disease or whether it could be a symptom.

A 2002 study reported that the Alexander Technique may have sustained benefits for patients with Parkinson's disease.[13]

A recent study at Stanford University concluded that laughter stimulates the parts of our brain that use the "feel good" chemical messenger dopamine.

Check out Laughter Yoga-combines unconditional laughter with yogic breathing. The concept of Laughter Yoga is based on the scientific fact that the body can not differentiate between fake or real laughter. Clinical research proves that laughter lowers levels of stress hormones, epinephrine, cortisol, etc. in the blood. It fosters a hopeful and positive attitude and has a profound impact on the immune system. Look for a Laughter club in your community.

Osteoarthritis

The weight bearing joints and joints of the hands are most often affected by the degenerative changes associated with osteoarthritis. Osteoarthritis is the most common form of arthritis, a degenerative joint disease mainly afflicting the elderly. Over 40 million Americans have osteoarthritis including 80% of people over the age of 50. Osteoarthritis is caused when the cushioning cartilage in joints breaks down or wears away, causing pain and stiffness.

Exercise is important in both prevention and treatment of arthritis because unused joints tend to stiffen. Lack of exercise contributes since the cartilage has no blood supply of its own and depends on joint movement to pump nutrients through its tissues. Good posture is also important to prevent stiffness and crippling. Poor posture can cause body weight to be distributed unevenly, placing more stress on certain joints, thus resulting in unnecessary pain for the arthritic person.

What can help?

- It is very important to maintain an ideal weight. Being overweight means increased stress on the weight bearing joints
- Massage, acupuncture, and acupressure can help soothe arthritis symptoms by improving

circulation, reducing tension, and easing muscle pain

- Foot reflexology, reiki, therapeutic touch and pulsed electromagnetic therapy may help too
- Movement therapies like yoga, t'ai chi and qigong
- Herbs and spices that may help include ginger, turmeric, green tea and flaxseed

Glucosamine and chondroitin have been studied and used across Europe and Asia for more than two decades and are prescription drugs in several countries. Many studies on thousands of people have shown both glucosamine and chondroitin relieve osteoarthritis pain about as well as NSAIDS, such as ibuprofen, naproxen, and aspirin, but without the dangerous gastrointestinal and other side effects.[4]

Osteoarthritis of the Knee

Osteoarthritis of the knee—Osteo means bone, arthritis means joint damage and swelling.

Osteoarthritis of the knee often runs in families and has been shown to be twice as common in women as in men and usually occurs after the age of 50. Osteoarthritis is common in people who are overweight, especially middle aged women. Osteoarthritis leads to degeneration of the knee cartilage and can cause pain, swelling and reduced functionality of the knee.

What you can do

- Wear cushioned training shoes to act as shock absorbers
- Exercise is good for Osteoarthritis. Being more active can help you have less pain and move more easily
- Use a walking stick or poles to take weight off the knee and to improve balance
- Use hand rails when climbing stairs
- Get up and stretch everyday
- Learn and practice t'ai chi
- Strengthen your thigh muscles. [5] In a study of 265 men and women with knee osteoarthritis,

Mayo Clinic researchers found that those with the strongest thigh muscles had less knee pain and better physical function than those with the weakest

- Maintain ideal weight
- Use a heating lamp or hot water bottle for pain.
- Acupuncture
- Consider glucosamine/chondroitin (1,500 mg of glucosamine and 1,200 mg of chondroitin) daily to strengthen aging cartilage.

Chapter 5

Living Well

The human body is designed for movement. Without it the muscles atrophy, circulation slows down and bones begin to thin. There are many applications, techniques, therapies, and classes offered to help maintain good posture and balanced movement. You may choose to try more than one depending on your physical ability. Do what "feels" right to you.

"Life is like riding a bicycle, to keep your balance you must keep moving."
Albert Einstein

How Active Are You?

Preventing a fall should be one of the most important things you do to maintain your independence. Listed in this section are techniques, therapies, and devices proven to help with your strength, endurance, vitality and balance. *Don't be afraid to try something new. You just might love it!*

Would you like more energy?

Walking is a great way to increase your energy levels. Positive mental outlook – living in the present moment and letting go of worry, guilt, resentment and "I should have's." Laughter is an instant energizer. Practice daily deep diaphragmatic breathing.

Here's to your health!

Dr. Robert E. Wear, exercise physiologist at the University of New Hampshire writes, "When the elderly exercise, their appearance improves, energy reserves increase, they eat better, their peripheral circulation improves, and their range of motion increases. There's tremendous difference in their vigor and vitality and they're much less likely to suffer the catastrophic falls that older people are prone to."

Whole Body Vibration

Whole body vibration technology was developed by the Russian Cosmonauts in an effort to combat muscle atrophy, prevent bone density loss and blood clotting during extended periods at zero gravity. The motion of the vibration platform causes the brain to tell the muscles to actively contract to maintain equilibrium. You can sit, stand or lie on the machine, which has a vibrating platform. The action of the vibration transmits energy through your body providing an invigorating workout.

Vibration therapy improves walk and balance in the elderly. "All older patients in nursing homes {except those with any contraindication} could benefit from whole body vibration", says study researcher Dr. Olivier Bruyere (University of Liege, Liege, Belgium)

A study [4] of 42 volunteers in a nursing home were separated into either a vibration group or a non-treatment group for a period of 6 weeks. The treatment group spent four 1-minute series, 3 times a week, plus 10 minutes a day of classical physical exercise.

After 6 weeks of therapy, the nursing home patients in the vibrating group showed:

- 143% improvement in physical function
- 41% improvement in pain relief

- 60% increase in vitality
- 23% improvement in general health
- 57% improvement in quality of walking as assessed by the Tinetti test (compared with a 2% improvement in control subjects)
- 77% improvement in equilibrium (compared with 1% worsening in controls).
- 39% decrease in time required to get up and go (compared with an increase in 14% among controls)

Even though this was a small study, "after just 3 weeks (or 9 sessions), we saw a great improvement in get-up-and-go." Dr. Bruyere tells *Rheumawire*

Fitness Benefits

- Weight loss-by increasing lean muscle mass
- Tone and firm-hundreds of muscle contractions per minute create an effective workout to tone muscles and increase circulation to help tighten skin
- Improves flexibility, range of motion, balance, and mobility
- The vibration causes your muscles to react to imbalance, strengthening muscles while increasing flexibility in muscles, joints, and ligaments
- Helps fight cellulite accumulation by toning muscles and increasing lymphatic drainage

Health Benefits

- Helps increase bone mineral density to combat osteoporosis
- Enhances circulation and lymphatic drainage by cleansing toxic buildup from the body and increases oxygenation in the blood
- Reduces pain and stiffness-increases circulation, lymphatic drainage, and increases muscle strength. May alleviate symptoms of fibromyalgia, arthritis and other pain
- Elevates HGH and serotonin while decreasing cortisol

Therapy Benefits

- Neuromuscular re-education when applicable; such as with MS, CP, or after a stroke
- Rehabilitation from injury-re-strengthening muscles after injury, illness, or surgery

There have been worldwide scientific studies of whole body vibration systems that indicate high success rates in the treatment of osteoporosis.[5]

In just 10 minutes a day it is possible to complete a whole body workout by simply stepping on to a Whole Body Vibration Exercise Machine. Or, as shown below, place your feet on the vibrating plate to get a lower body workout.

Contraindications for use:
- Acute Thrombosis
- Artificial Joints {recent}
- Epilepsy

- Severe Migraines
- Pulmonary Embolism
- Pregnancy
- Tumors {cancerous}
- Head injuries, Known Neurological Conditions
- Recent wounds from an Operation or Surgery
- Recently Placed IUD's, Metal Pins, or Plates
- Retinal Detachment, Known Retinal Conditions
- Serious Cardiovascular Disease
- Acute Hernia, Discopathy, or Spondylosis
- Type 1 Diabetes
- Pacemaker and Implantable Cardioverter Defibrillator

If you have any condition listed above consult a physician or physical therapist before using. User weight must not exceed 330lbs.

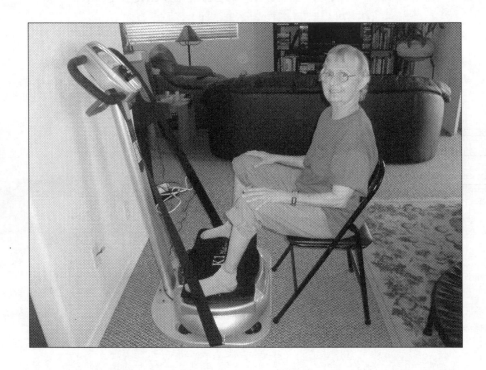

To view testimonials on the benefits of the K-1 for seniors, go to www.k1wholebodyvibration.com/testimonial_video.aspx or if interested in purchasing go to www.stopfallsez.com

The Morter March

Start your day with a few repetitions of The Morter March, developed by chiropractor Ted Morter. What may seem like a miniature version of aerobic exercise, The Morter March helps increase heart rate, deepen breathing, and strengthen muscles. The movements are deliberate and smooth which gives the added benefit of improved balance. The Morter March helps to improve neurological balance and internal communication.

Follow these instructions
- Stand comfortably erect
- Step forward with your right foot, keeping your left foot flat
- Bend your right knee, so you can't see your toes
- Stretch your left arm up to 45 degrees
- Stretch your right arm down and back to 45 degrees
- Turn your head toward your raised arm, close your eyes (unless you are unsteady) and stretch
- Hold your breath10 seconds
- Exhale and reverse the process with your left foot forward and right arm up
- If you are unsteady practice next to a wall

- Repeat 4-5 times, and do twice a day for best results

Benefits

- Improves muscular and neurological balance
- Restores symmetry to joints
- Improves coordination and stamina
- Stretches, strengthens and balances muscle tone

Exercise

Build strength in your legs through exercise.

"Now the evidence is overwhelming that exercise and a long, healthy life go hand in hand" states Dr. N.P. Napalkov, World Health Organization assistant Director General.

Statistics from the National Institutes of Health show that 58% of adult Americans get little or no exercise. Most people do not realize that lack of exercise is responsible for nearly one third of all deaths.

Walking is an "antioxidant nutrient" and one of the best forms of exercise for your health. It is simple, free and helps keep your weight in check. Walking 30 minutes a day while adding deep breathing can help:

- improve muscle tone
- cleanse your circulatory system
- increase heart strength

Besides helping with your cardiovascular system you will obtain vitamin D from sunlight. **Walking, riding your bike or jogging all increase both muscle and bone mass.** Walking regularly lowers your risk of falls, especially worrisome for older women.

If you don't exercise, not only do you lose muscle, you'll lose up to 1% of your bone mass every year. Plus, exercise is a great mood enhancer, giving you a greater sense of well being.

- Exercise stimulates metabolism, especially before you eat, to aid weight loss
- Exercise uses up stored body fat. Calories are burned at a greater pace for several hours after you exercise
- Exercise stimulates circulation, lowering blood pressure and helping to prevent heart disease by increasing blood flow

Did you know that disease often results from an under active body? When you exercise oxygen and nutrients are transported to your cells while it carries away toxins and wastes to elimination organs. Numerous studies have shown physical fitness reduces falls. The more fit a person is, if a fall occurs, the less likely they are to sustain a serious injury.

Rolfing

Rolfing is the commonly used name for the system of structural integration soft tissue manipulation founded by Ida Pauline Rolf in the 1950's. She spent 50 years of study and refinement while working with her own children to help improve their body structure and health.

Rolfing helps to achieve balance and improve body posture. Methods involve the use of stretching, deep tissue massage, and relaxation techniques to loosen old injuries and break bad movement posture patterns, which can cause long-term health and body stress.

Rolfing practitioners use the elbows, fingers, and knuckles to stretch and open fascia to help correct the habitual patterns of misalignment in the head, shoulders, abdomen, pelvis and legs. By correcting these habitual patterns practitioners can:

- Help improve posture and conditions caused by poor posture
- Helps relieve muscle pain and tension, especially in the neck, upper back and lower back
- Improves flexibility and coordination
- Develops greater alertness and vitality

Sessions are done privately. Basic Rolfing programs usually start with 10 sessions lasting 60-90 minutes each.

Alexander Technique

The Alexander Technique can help end improper use of the neuromuscular system and bring body posture back into balance, as well as, eliminate psycho-physical interferences, helps release long-held tension, and aids in re-establishing muscle tone.

The Alexander Technique was developed by Australian Mathias Alexander in the early 1900's. He was an actor who recognized that vocal and throat problems were related to tension and stress in the way he held his body. With instruction, the Alexander Technique can clear a client of bad habits by directing his or her body to stand, sit, lie and walk correctly. His method helps improve balance and flexibility by showing people how to recognize their postural problems and to stand and move with more ease.

The Alexander Technique can help if you suffer from,
- A stiff neck and shoulder
- Back pain
- Carpal tunnel syndrome
- Repetitive strain injury
- Or if you are an actor, singer, musician, dancer or athlete who is not performing well

Benefits include:

- More comfortable and erect posture
- Easier and healthier breathing
- Increased vitality and strength
- Relief from chronic strain and pain

Individual one-on-one sessions are best, but there are group classes available. A 2002 study reported that the Alexander Technique may have sustained benefits for patients with Parkinson's disease. [6]

Stretching

Stretching – Why stretch? Because it keeps muscles supple, prepares you for movement, feels good and allows you to go from inactivity to vigorous activity without strain. Stretching is easy but must be done correctly to prevent harming the body. So in the beginning take it easy.

- Warm up before stretching - walk or do mild exercise for 5 minutes
- Hold each stretch for at least 30 seconds. It takes time to lengthen tissues safely
- Breathe slowly, deeply, naturally, and exhale as you bend forward
- Don't bounce! Bouncing can cause small tears in the muscles, tightening them even further
- Stretching should be pain free - Go to the point where you feel mild tension then relax and hold the stretch
- Maintains flexibility and improves the range of motion of your joints which helps keep you in better balance and less prone to falls
- Stretching improves circulation, promotes better posture, helps relieve stress and it just feels good
- Stretch before you go to bed to help insure muscle relaxation and better rest

- Stretch in the morning to oxygenate your tissues, limber your body and help clear and clean it from the previous nights waste

If you maintain good flexibility throughout your life you can avoid the problems that go with tight muscles, bad posture, and stiff joints. This may be one of the worst problems of getting older, the loss in range of motion. Stretching is one of the best ways to stay limber.

Stretch whenever you feel like it! Drink plenty of water! Your muscles stretch more easily when your body is properly hydrated.

Dance Lessons

If you're tired of the treadmill and looking for a fun way to stay fit and healthy, it may be time to take a dance class! Dancing can give you a great mind-body workout. There's even chair dancing for those with physical limitations. [1] A 2003 study published in the New England Journal of Medicine found that ballroom dancing at least twice a week made people less likely to develop dementia.

Dancing can help:
- strengthen bones and muscles without hurting your joints
- tone your entire body
- improve your posture and balance, which can prevent falls
- increase your stamina and flexibility
- reduce stress and tension
- build confidence
- provide opportunities to meet people
- ward off illnesses like diabetes, high blood pressure, heart disease, osteoporosis, and depression

Dancing can burn between 200 and 400 calories, about as many as walking, swimming, or riding a bike. For example, the side-to-side movements of square dancing can help to strengthen weight bearing bones in the knees and hips without injuring joints.

Try ballroom, square dancing, flamenco, west coast swing, salsa or country western.

Poles for Balance & Mobility

Do you like to take walks or do you enjoy hiking? How about just getting more exercise? Poles for balance and mobility may help you navigate more safely. The poles are light weight and easy to use, giving a sense of balanced movement.

Using Poles may benefit by:

- Reducing stress on your knees, ankles, hips and spine
- Improving posture and endurance
- Reduce the risk of falling
- Improve upper body strength, engaging the pectorals, back, triceps and abdominal muscles
- Increase heart rate and provide greater aerobic output
- Help with weight loss and with navigating tricky terrain

Poles for balance and mobility provide stability and a sense of security, especially in people with Parkinson's, MS, Peripheral Neuropathy, Arthritis, Alzheimer's, Osteoporosis, and Spinal Stenosis.[2]

For more information go to www.polesformobility.com

Assistive Devices

Don't let pride keep you from having a full life.

Use an **assistive device** to help with balance and stability - walker, cane, etc.

Walkers, canes, scooters and wheelchairs can reduce the risk of falling; however, when used improperly these aids are also associated with an increase of falls, like not setting a brake on a walker or wheelchair. Many seniors do not want to use an assistive device because of the fear of their being stigmatized as old, frail, loss of independence, etc.

Always use some kind of assistive device when taking medication that affects your balance.

Contact your health care provider to be medically assessed before choosing a particular assistive device. If it's expensive, borrow or rent one to see if it meets your needs before you buy it. Check out the yellow pages for rentals and sales. Also check with your local Salvation Army or Goodwill for used assistive devises.

Feldenkrais

The Feldenkrais Method was developed by distinguished scientist and educator Moshe Feldenkrais (1904-1984). While playing soccer, Feldenkrais suffered a serious knee injury. Doctors told him he had a 50% chance of recovery or he would be confined to a wheelchair for the rest of his life. Not satisfied with the prognosis and treatments available Feldenkrais set out to explore the connection between mind and body to help improve physical movement and function. For 40 years Feldenkrais developed an ingenious method for effective neuromuscular re-education. People with orthopedic or neurological problems experienced wonderful therapeutic benefits.

Feldenkrais takes you on an internal journey to rediscover your
- agility
- balance
- flexibility
- coordination

Feldenkrais is for all levels and ages, and allows you to go at your own pace, creating a deeper sense of how you move and better awareness in general.

"I recommend the Feldenkrais Method to patients whose movement has been restricted by injury, cerebral palsy, stroke, fibromyalgia or chronic pain. I also believe that the Feldenkrais Method can help all of us feel more comfortable in our bodies" Andrew Weil, MD, Best Selling Author of Spontaneous Healing.

Available in group or individual classes

Water Aerobics

Water Aerobics - Perform water aerobics to improve lower body strength. The body is almost weightless in water, which makes it ideal for increasing lower body strength, power and agility. Most of the routines are done in waist-deep or chest-deep water. A basic routine will teach you arm and leg movements that progress in frequency, intensity, duration, and intricacy. Although considered aerobic, for cardiovascular fitness, aerobic water exercise also improves:

- Strength
- Flexibility
- Balance
- Muscular Endurance

Chiropractic

Chiropractic means "done with the hands". Chiropractic therapy uses physical manipulation of the spine to relieve pain and return energy to the body. Treatments include soft tissue, spinal and body adjustments to align and free up the spine and nervous system of interference or blockage. Chiropractic adjustments help prevent wear and tear on the joints and ligaments by maintaining their proper positioning. More benefits include:

- Improved overall health and immunity
- More energy and better quality sleep
- Increased mobility and range of motion
- Improved spinal structure
- Aligned and healthier spinal disks
- Improved posture
- Relief from stress and tension
- Arthritic joint pain relief
- Increased joint health
- Decreased tissue inflammation

Chiropractic does not address disease through drugs or chemicals, but by locating and adjusting a musculoskeletal area of the body which is functioning improperly.

An alternative to conventional chiropractic care, the B.E.S.T (Bio Energetic Synchronization Technique) method utilizes a non forceful chiropractic technique that removes interference from the nervous system by the use of hands. Developed in the mid 70's by chiropractor Milton Ted Morter Jr., the B.E.S.T. method is a holistic program that coordinates and balances the workings of all systems of the body and is used to re-establish the full healing potential.

Massage Therapy

Massage Therapy dates back thousands of years and is one of the oldest and simplest forms of therapy. The main goal of massage therapy is to help the body heal itself and to increase health and well being. There are many different techniques but in general therapists press, rub, and otherwise manipulate the muscles and other soft tissues of the body. Massage aids in loosening and relaxing stiffened muscles, improves flexibility of the joints and makes the body more capable of a wider range of movements.

George Burns and Bob Hope had weekly massages and both lived a 100 years!

Some of the many health benefits are:
- Improved posture
- Strengthened immune system
- Helps relieve headache pain
- Relieves tension
- Improves breathing and flexibility
- Relaxes muscles and helps manage pain
- Helps lower blood pressure
- Improves circulation
- Encourages relaxation
- Relieves stress

Familiar and popular forms of massage are:
- Sports Massage
- Deep Tissue Massage
- Trigger Point Massage
- Swedish massage
- Reflexology which applies pressure to the feet

Physical Therapy

"Falling and fear of falling among seniors is a public health problem and should not be accepted simply as a normal condition of aging," says physical therapist Leslie Allison, PT, PhD, [3]

According to the American Physical Therapy Association, falling and fear of falling may be reduced by physical therapist intervention. Physical therapists ("PTs") use specially designed exercises and equipment to help patients regain or improve their physical abilities. PTs use a wide variety of techniques to help decrease stiffness and pain, improve mobility, motion and strength. PTs screen, examine, evaluate, diagnose and determine a plan of care for patients. If you have existing balance problems, PTs can examine your medical history and design an individualized program of exercise and activities.

Their specific program will help with
- The ability to move
- Reduce pain
- Restore function and range of motion
- Improve strength, flexibility and proper gait
- Wellness, fitness and mobility

Remaining physically active as one gets older is one of the most important things seniors can do to prevent falls. Half of older adults think that reducing their physical activity level will lessen their risk of falls when the opposite is true.

Rebounding - Mini Trampoline with Support Bar

(recommended)

Rebounding is one of the best all-around exercises. Rebounding strengthens the whole body instead of concentrating on one muscle group. It's convenient and can be done in the privacy of your own home or office.

When we rebound, we increase the pull of gravity on our bodies. As a result, the gravitational forces condition, tone and strengthen each body cell. Rebounding exercise is excellent for our senior citizens, those physically handicapped, those who are recuperating from an accident or injury, or anyone else who needs exercise but is hampered by a pre-existing physical condition.

A Phoenix newspaper reported: "Esther Delana Lewis celebrated her 100th birthday dancing a jig on the mini trampoline in her home. It does wonders for my health," she said. "Esther sings and dances" on her rebound unit several times a day. What's really interesting about Esther is she could hardly walk when she started rebounding. She usually had to use a wheelchair. (*Looking Good Feeling Great* by Karol Kuhm Truman)

Rebounding exercise can be adapted to any level of fitness; and it's good for most anyone with physical limitations. A quality unit can cushion the trauma to the joints up to 85%

while the person is rebounding. Beginners can start just by walking on their unit. If you can't walk at all, place your feet on the rebounder while another person jumps up and down on it for the therapeutic benefits.

- Always start slowly—give your cells a chance to "warm up", and to become accustomed to the stress you're putting on them
- Talk to your doctor, especially if you have any questions concerning your physical and health status
- Keep your balance, use a steady bounce and find something stationary to look at. This helps you keep a point of focus, plus you will have better equilibrium

"Rebounding allows the muscles to go through a full range of motion at equal force. It helps people to learn to shift their weight properly and to be aware of body positions and balance." Dr. James White, PhD., UCSD

As a bonus, rebounding is wonderful for chronically constipated people. The steady bounce sets up a pulsating rhythm transmitted by the nervous system to the brain area responsible for regulating the intestinal system, which re-establishes one's rhythmical bowel activity. Digestion is improved too.

Dr. Morton Walker writes "Cellercise" or rebounding, tends to stop premature aging. The effects of hardening of the arteries are reversed, prevented or diminished.

"Rebound (Cellercise) exercise is the closest thing to the Fountain of Youth that science has discovered. We found that jumping on good (Cellercise) equipment is effective in improving the symptoms of over 80% of the patients reporting to our rehabilitation lab." Dr. James White, PhD., UCSD

Gait Training

Gait training refers to helping a patient relearn to walk safely and efficiently. Gait training is usually done by rehabilitation specialists who evaluate the abnormalities in the person's gait and employ such treatments as strengthening and balance training to improve stability and body perception as these pertain to the patient's environment.

Human gait is measured from heel strike to heel strike, also known as the gait cycle or "one stride". A person's gait is a pattern of stepping or walking that is specific to that individual. People usually need gait training if there is some lower trunk or lower limb dysfunction.

Gait training may be needed if
- You have muscle weakness
- Deformity
- Loss of sensation
- Pain in the weight bearing joints
- Osteoarthritis
- Muscular dystrophy
- Muscle atrophy
- Neurological or orthopedic impairment

Gait training sometimes incorporates the use of assistive devices such as parallel bars, walkers, or canes.

Chapter 6

Your Senses

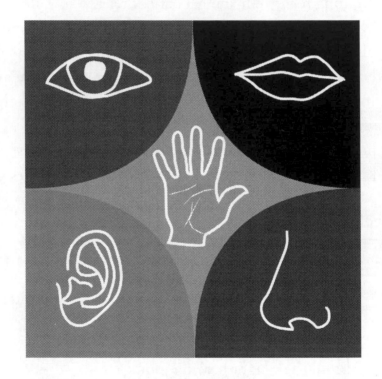

*This section covers obvious changes that occur as we age
and the role they play in relationship to our balance.*

**Take care of your body.
It's the only place you have to live.**

~ Jim Rohn

As we age, our senses, which give us vital information about the world around us, change. This is most often from environmental factors. Of the five senses, (taste, smell, hearing, touch, and vision) the two that are usually the most affected are vision and hearing, but fortunately modern equipment such as glasses and hearing aids are available.

Good nutrition, increased activity, and being optimistic can contribute to an improved quality of life.

Remember that in spite of physical loss and some difficulties, "most" older adults adjust just fine and are able to compensate for their sensory losses.

Vision

Almost everyone over 55 needs glasses at least part of the time. Fortunately only 15-20% of older people have bad enough vision to impair driving, and only 5% are unable to read. Vision plays a direct and very important role in balance by providing the nervous system with information regarding the positions and movements of body segments in relation to each other and the environment.

Research shows that impaired depth perception was the strongest risk factor for multiple falls. Subjects with good vision in both eyes had the lowest incidence of falls, whereas subjects with poor vision in one eye had elevated fall rates that were equivalent to those of patients with moderate or poor vision in both eyes. Strategies to maximize vision in both eyes may be particularly beneficial in preventing falls. (Lord et al., 2002)

Multi-focal Glasses & Falls

Although using a single pair of glasses is more convenient, studies show that bifocal, trifocal, or progressive lens glasses may have some disadvantages for seniors because the lower lenses blur floor-level objects at critical distances for detecting environmental hazards.[1] (Lord et al., 2002) Clean eye glasses often to improve visibility.

A diet high in sugar and refined carbohydrates can be a major eye offender, causing a more than 300% increase in the risk of vision problems.

Green tea may help protect eyes against harmful oxidative stress. A study published in The Journal of Agriculture and Food Chemistry, shows that green tea catechins (anti-oxidants such as vitamin C, vitamin E, lutein and zeaxanthin) absorb into the lens, retina and other eye tissues and may help protect against diseases such as glaucoma.[2]

Dark greens like spinach, collard greens and kale are excellent in preventing age-related macular degeneration. Eat your greens everyday!

Hearing

Have your hearing checked regularly. The National Institute of Health estimates that one-third of Americans between the ages of 65 & 75 and close to one-half of those older than 75 have some degree of hearing loss. The loss appears to be caused by a decrease in the elasticity of the ear drum.

Your ears not only help you hear, they help you maintain your balance. Your equilibrium is controlled in a portion of the inner ear. Fluid and small hairs in the semicircular canal stimulate the nerve that helps the brain maintain balance. As you age, your ear structure can deteriorate. Another cause of impaired hearing is impacted ear wax, which can be removed by your doctor.

Hearing may also decline slightly if you were exposed to a lot of loud noise when younger. When you must be around loud noise, either at work or at play, use something to protect your hearing, like headphones.

More than 50 million Americans suffer from Tinnitus and 80% of people with hearing problems have it. Tinnitus means "ringing in the ears." To help reduce ringing in the ears, try massaging your neck, ear and temples. Pull the earlobes to the top of your ear and back down to help clear passages of excess wax or mucous. Do this several times.

Chiropractic adjustments, acupuncture, and shiatsu massage may be helpful for both tinnitus and vertigo. Also consider a series of cranial sacral massage treatments from a good massage therapist, which also helps with TMJ (temperomandibular joint syndrome) a painful, arthritis-like syndrome causing headaches, ringing in the ears, popping of the jaw joint, sinus pain, hearing loss and dizziness.

Touch

As we get older our sense of touch changes, mainly because the skin's sensitivity decreases. With less sensitivity older people become less responsive to stimuli affecting the sense of touch.

Did you know walking barefoot thickens the skin covering the sensors in the foot and causes a decrease in sensitivity?

Our sense of touch is a very powerful stimulation. It allows us to stay in touch with our surroundings and to complete everyday tasks.

With reduced ability to detect vibration, pressure and touch, there is an increase in the risk of injuries. It is possible to develop problems with walking because of reduced ability to perceive where your body is in relation to the floor.

Take control of your health by managing your lifestyle. Research suggests that good lifestyle choices including exercise, diet and nutrition have significant impact on how well we age.

Chapter 7

Body, Mind & Spirit

Want more clarity, lessening of stress and a general sense of well being? What about better posture and breathing habits? You can have all this and much more through a Body, Mind & Spirit practice.

"The three together - body, mind and spirit - cooperate to produce the most profound medicine ever known, and it is found right within you."
~ Dr. Roger Jahnke

T'ai Chi

T'ai Chi is an ancient Chinese discipline that has been practiced for centuries throughout China and around the world. T'ai Chi employs movements that are slow and non-strenuous. In fact, it's gentle movements' help the body strengthen bone mass and connective tissue, and is lower impact than even brisk walking.

The purpose of T'ai Chi is to generate, circulate and balance the body energy or chi, which results in improved circulation, breathing, flexibility, balance, and coordination. Research has proven that it lowers blood pressure and reduces stress and tension. T'ai Chi is a lifelong practice, and no one quits because they get "too old". You don't need to be in good physical shape or even be currently physically active to start practicing T'ai Chi.

Growing evidence shows that Qigong and T'ai Chi practices could be some of the best forms of physical activity for diverse populations because these activities are low impact, low cost and relatively easy to learn.

A study through Harvard, Yale and Emory Universities stunned researchers when they discovered that the gentle, slow, relaxing, low impact T'ai Chi improved the balance of practitioners profoundly, reducing their risk of falling by 47.5%.[1]

More scientific studies have shown that T'ai Chi works magic on health and improves conditions such as:

- Arthritis
- Osteoporosis
- Heart disease
- Diabetes
- Respiration disease and other chronic diseases
- Increases maximum oxygen consumption
- Increases immune function

T'ai Chi might well be called "Medication in Motion", as there is growing evidence that this mind body practice has value in treating and preventing many health problems. Harvard Health Publication May 2009[3]

Do you have arthritis pain? In a study described in the Journal of Nursing Scholarship, researchers at Case Western Reserve University found that one hour of T'ai Chi a week may have significantly reduced chronic arthritis pain in a group of older adults. T'ai Chi may help to reduce arthritis pain by increasing circulation and stimulating repair of damaged joints.

Scientists say T'ai Chi may curb shingles.[2] Researchers have found that older people who perform the graceful movements of T'ai Chi have a better immune response against the virus that causes shingles. (Study funded by the National Institute of Aging)

To find a T'ai Chi class in your community, try the following:

- Community college
- Y.M.C.A.
- Senior centers

- Community centers
- Local hospitals
- T'ai Chi or yoga studio

Talk to the instructor and see if you can watch a class. This will help you make a decision about whether its right for you.

Qigong

The Grandmother of all Traditional Chinese Medicines, Qigong dates back several thousand years. It is an ancient system of energetic movement, body positioning, meditation and breathing methods that have been developed to strengthen the body, stimulate the flow of blood and improve the circulation of Qi, the energy of life that flows through all living things. Qigong builds strength, stamina and clears the mind. Qigong can be done by anyone, regardless of age or physical condition. Much of Qigong can be modified to sitting, standing or even lying down to help open and unify the body. The major benefit is in the way it helps to regulate the nervous system and improve brain function, contributing to stress relief and relaxation.

T'ai Chi Easy™

Based on the book The Healer Within, written by Roger Jahnke, O.M.D., T'ai Chi Easy™ utilizes the Vitality Enhancement Method (Bu Zheng Qigong) along with a modified T'ai Chi set, plus self-care methods to support and empower individuals in their quest for improved health. These modified T'ai Chi movements, breathing exercises, self massage methods and use of meditation help enhance one's life energy and increase the bodies capacity to heal itself. The entire program can be done sitting, standing or even lying down. Very easy!

Health benefits of T'ai Chi Easy™ include:

- Stress relief
- Improved balance
- Cardiovascular health
- Heightened immunity
- Greater mental focus
- Alleviation and reduction of chronic pain

T'ai Chi Easy™ classes are great for seniors and people with physical limitations. Look for a T'ai Chi Easy™ facilitator in your area by visiting www.taichieasy.org.

Water T'ai Chi

Water T'ai Chi is performed in chest deep water kept at a temperature near 90 degrees and is done in an upright position. Water T'ai Chi combines the principles of water fitness and the graceful flowing movements of T'ai Chi, enhancing not only the body, but the mind and spirit as well. Most find the exercises improve strength, flexibility, balance, coordination and posture. In addition, participants develop grace and powerful use of the whole body. If you lose your balance there is no risk.

Ai Chi

Ai Chi, is also done in the water, with temperatures ranging from 88-96 degrees. Ai Chi is great for anyone who would like to improve their balance. The movements are slow, fluid and the body is relaxed. Deep diaphragmatic breathing is incorporated, which gives a feeling of well being. Hydrostatic pressure increases blood circulation, boosts oxygenation of all organs and muscles to promote healing. Ai Chi helps improve muscle tone, flexibility and range of motion. Other benefits include reducing symptoms of connective tissue, joint and muscular ailments.

Yoga

Yoga is one of the best bodywork techniques to harmonize body, mind and spirit. Yoga is a great technique to open up blockages and balance the energies in the body. When practicing, priority should be given to effective breathing techniques that are synchronized with each movement. Yoga works all the major muscle groups, including the hips, thighs, abdominals, arms and back. It will physically improve strength and flexibility. On a mental level yoga sharpens focus and concentration.

Studies have shown that yoga helps relieve pain in those with arthritis and fibromyalgia. Yoga also helps to lower high blood pressure and improves digestion.

Some of the most popular forms of Yoga include Hatha, Vinyasa, Ashtanga, Iyengae and Birkram. If you are a beginner, you might want to try Hatha or Vinyasa. Call your local Y.M.C.A., community centers or private yoga studios.

Epilogue

Practicing T'ai Chi on a daily basis has added immeasurable quality to my life. Besides the physical benefits{lower body strength, great balance, flexibility and coordination}, I have learned to slow down and enjoy the peace, tranquility, and beauty this wonderful life has to offer. Learning to live in the moment and enjoy who I am. What a blessing!

In this book I have given simple steps to use in regard to fall prevention. I hope that each reader takes their health or their loved ones' health and vitality seriously. The risk of falls is great and there are many factors that contribute to falls. But if we are aware of them and take action, our chance of having a longer more fulfilling life is greater.

I wish you a rich, long life filled with love, hugs, joy and lots of laughter!

Namaste',
Roxanne

Namaste'—The Divine Spirit in me honors the Divine Spirit in you.

Disclaimer

This book is for informational purposes only and is educational in nature. Statements in this book are not intended to diagnose, treat, cure or prevent disease.

Neither the authors nor the publisher shall be liable or responsible for any loss or risk which incurred as a consequence of the use or application of any of the contents of this book. This publication is not intended to be a replacement for advice from a qualified health care professional.

About the Author

I am in regular contact with Roxanne's clients and without fail each conversation includes praises for her. Her class members feel her compassion and commitment and look forward to attending classes because they have fun. Having fun, and feeling as a part of a bonded group, is of key importance for people living with a chronic, progressive disease. Roxanne's students benefit from this and therefore feel they are taking part in managing their disease.

I am currently the Recreation Therapy Coordinator for the Muhammad Ali Parkinson Center, an entity of the Barrow Neurological Institute and St. Joseph's Hospital and Medical Center. Roxanne has taught people with Parkinson's and has been committed to reading and learning about the disease, plus hands on experience. She is self motivated and self directed.

Darolyn O'Donnell, CTRS, MS.

References

Chapter 1

1. CDC Non fatal Fall-related Injuries Associated with Dogs and Cats United States, March 27, 2009/58{11};277-281

Chapter 2

1. The Surgeon General's Report on Nutrition and Health 1988 US Department of Health and Human Services Public Health Service DHHS {PHS} Publication No. 88-50210
2. Bruce Hollis-Autoimmune Rev.2010 Sept;9{11}:709-15. Epub2010Jul1.
3. American Geriatrics Society's 2005 meeting to Highlight Latest Research and Report on Growing Shortage of Geriatricians Orlando, Fl. May 11,2005 A Higher Dose of Vitamin D Reduces Risk of Falls
4. Hip Fractures and Fluoridation in Utah's Elderly Population, a study by C. Danielson et al [JAMA, Aug 12, 1992.268:746-8
5. Calcium loss, fracture due to animal protein By Tessa Salazar Phillippine Daily Inquirer July 17,2009 INQUIRER. NET

6. The influence of Vibration on Bone Mineral Density in Women Who Have Weak Bones After Menopause April 7,2010 ClinicalTrials.gov id:NCT00420940

7. Aqueous extract of valerian root{Valeriana Officinalis L.} improves sleep quality in man. Pharmacol Biochem Behav. 1982 Jul;17{1};65-71

8. Effects of L-tryptophan (a natural sedative) on human sleep. Wyatt R, et al. Lance 1970;842-846

9. Troen et al. B-vitamin deficiency causes hyperhomocysteinemia and vascular cognitive impairment in mice. Proceedings of the National Academy of Sciences, 2008; 105 {34} : 12474 Dol:

10. AM J Public Health. 1997; 87: 992-997

11. Dairy-product intake and hip fracture among older women: issues for health behavior. Psychol Rep 1999 Oct; 85 (2) 423-30

12. Journal of the American Geriatrics Society (Volume 53, Issue 11)

Chapter 2 Recommended Reading

• Blaylock Russell, M.D. "Excitotoxins: The Taste That Kills," Health Press, Santa Fe 1994

• Cleary Larry M.C. Dr. "The Brain Trust Program" 2007

• Permutter David, M.D., FACN & Carol Colman " The Better Brain Book" 2004

• Page Linda, Ph.D., 12th Edition Healthy Healing A Guide to Self Healing For Everyone 2004

• Pelton Ross, LaValle James B., Hawkins Ernest B., Krinsky Daniel Drug-Induced Nutrient Depletion Handbook 2001

Chapter 2 Resource Links

www.pentawater.com
www.kegel-exercises.com
www.braggs.com
www.NoFluoride.com

Chapter 3

1. Going Barefoot in Home May Contribute to Elderly Falls-Science Daily {June 23,2010}
2. Journal of Aging and Physical Activity, 11{4} 487-501 2005/07/24 13:35:39 GMT-6

Chapter 4

1. Rittweger J and Felsenbert D Resistive vibration exercise prevents bone loss during 8 weeks of strict bed rest in health male subjects: results from the Berlin Bed Rest {BBR} study, 26th Annual Meeting of the American Society of Bone and Mineral Research: October 1-5, 2004; Seattle, Wa; Presentation 1145
2. Hackney ME, Earhart GM, T'ai Chi improves balance and mobility in people with Parkinson's Disease, Gait Posture {2008} , doi:10.1016/j.gaitpost.2008.02.005
3. Whole Body Vibration verses conventional physiotherapy to improve balance and gait in Parkinson's disease. Arch Phys Med Rehavil. 2008;89(3):399-403
4. Nutraceuticals as therapeutic agents in osteoarthritis. The role of glucosamine, chondroitin sulfate, and collagen hydrolysate Rheum Dis Clin North Am. 1999 May;25 (2):379-95
5. Mayo Clinic {2006, December 27} Stronger Leg Muscles Can Protect Against Knee Osteoarthritis. Science Daily

6. Resnicow K, Barone J, Engle A, et al: Diet and serum lipids in vegan vegetarians: A model for risk reduction. J Am Diet Assoc 1991:91:447-53

7. Changes in local myocardial blood circulation following oral administration of Crataegus extract in non-narcotized dogs. Arneimittelforschung. 1974 May:24{5}:783-785

8. McCarron DA and Morris CD: Epidemiological evidence associating dietary calcium and calcium metabolism with blood pressure. Am Nephrol 6 Supplement 1:3-9, 1986 Whelton PK and, Klag J: magnesium and blood pressure: Review of epidemiologic and clinical trial experience. Am J cardiol 63:26 G-30G,1989

9. J Am Geriatr Soc. 2005 Dec;53(12):2106-11. Late-life anemia is associated with increased risk of recurrent falls.

10. Prevalence of vitamin D insufficiency in patients with Parkinson's disease and Alzheimer disease Arch Neurol 2008 Oct;65 (10): 1348-52

11. Petkov V; plants with hypotensive, antiatheromatous and coronarodilating action. Am J Chin Med 7:197-236,1979

12. Fibrinolytic and antithrombotic action of bromelain may eliminate thrombosis in heart patients. Med Hypotheses. 1980 Nov; 6(11):1123-33.

13. 13) A 2002 study reported that the Alexander Technique may have sustained benefits for patients with Parkinson's disease. AM SAT News/summer 2010/Issue N 83

Chapter 4 Recommended Reading

- Bragg Paul C. N.D., Ph.D. and Bragg, Patricia N.D., Ph.D. Healthy Heart
- Murray Michael T. N.D. Natural Alternatives to Over-the-counter and Prescription Drugs
- Perlmutter, MD., FACN, Coleman Carol The Better Brain Book. In this book, written by neurologist Dr. Perlmutter, you will find both conventional and alternative care.

Chapter 4 Resources

www.maprc.com
www.stopfallsez.com

Chapter 5 References

1. Use It or Lose It---Do Effortless Mental Activities Protect Against Dementia? June 19,2003 Coyle J.T. N Engl Jmed 2003, 348:2489-2490
2. Effects of Walking Poles on Lower Extremity Gait Mechanics Med SciSports Exerc. 2001Jan;33 (1):142-7
3. Effects of sensory-challenge balance exercise program on multi sensory reweighting and clinical balance measures in the fall-prone elderly. Allison, L.K. Jeka, J.J., Kiemel, T.&K foury-House L.M.
4. Controlled whole body vibration to decrease fall risk and improve health-related quality of life of nursing home residents. Arch Phys Med Rehabil. 2005Feb; 86 (2):303-7
5. Low-frequency vibratory exercise reduces the risk of bone fracture more than walking: a randomized controlled trial. Gusi N, Raimundo A, Leal A.

6. A 2002 study reported that the Alexander Technique may have sustained benefits for patients with Parkinson's disease. AM SAT News/summer2010/Issue N 83

Chapter 5 Recommended Reading

- Truman Kuhm Karol, Looking Good Feeling Great 1982

Chapter 5 Resource Links

www.polesformobility.com
www.rolf.org
www.alexandertechnique.com
www.feldenkrais.com

Chapter 6 References

1. The Falls and Balance Research Group directed by Professor Stephen Lord, www.neura.edu.au/health/falls-balance
2. Journal of Agriculture and Food Chemistry Published online ahead of print: DOI:10.1021/jf9032602 Title: Green Tea Catechins and Their Oxidative Protection in the Rat Eye Authors C.Pui Pang et al

Chapter 7 References

1. Harvard Health Letter Volume 21 number 11-September 1996 Issue 20th Anniversary Year
2. In Harmony For Health-Graceful T'ai Chi Appears to Boost Immunity, Including Helping Elderly Fend Off Shingles April 24,2007 by Melissa Healy Los Angeles Times
3. Harvard Medical Schools Harvard Health Publication, May, 2009

Chapter 7 Resource Links

www.taichichih.org
www.nqa.org
www.yoga.com
www.IIQTC.com
www.taichieasy.org